FOLENS SCIENCE BOOK 3

Simon Smith
Carolyn Dale
Sarah Galpin
Jo Powell
Sue Stalley
Pat Szczesniak

Series Consultant
Dr Anne Whitehead

Acknowledgements

The authors and publishers would like to thank the following for supplying photographs.

Alcan Europe Limited 17

Holt Studios International Nigel Cattlin 41, 42, 46, 48 (2), Bob Gibbons 42, Primrose Peacock 34, 38 (2), 39, 41, Inga Spence 46 (3)

Mary Evans Picture Library 12, 63

Natural Science Photos 30

Oxford Scientific Films G.I. Bernard 30, Scott Camazine 31, Martin Chillmaid 41, Breck P. Kent 38, Richard Packwood 26, Ian West 26

Popperfoto 12

The Science Photo Library George Bernard 34, 39, Bsip Chassenet 30, Patrick Donehue 54, Pascal Goetgheluck 30, David Parker 34, 38, Francoise Sauze 60, Maximilian Stock Ltd. 47, David Nunuk 54, J.C. Revy 34, James Stevenson 31 (2),

Spectrum Colour Library 48, 54, 55, 56, 60 (2), 62

Telegraph Colour Library 33

Every effort has been made to trace the copyright holders, we apologise in advance for any unintentional omissions.

First published in 2001 by Folens Limited.

United Kingdom: Folens Publishers, Apex Business Centre, Boscombe Road, Dunstable LU5 4RL.
Email: folens@folens.com

Ireland: Folens Publishers, Greenhills Road, Tallaght, Dublin 24.
Email: info@folens.ie

Poland: JUKA, ul. Renesansowa 38, Warsaw 01-905.

Editor: Melody Eyers
Layout artist: James Brown
Cover design: Martin Cross
Illustrations: Alan Baker, Debbie Clark

British Library Cataloguing in Publication Data. A catalogue record for this publication is available from the British Library.

ISBN 1 84163 750-5

Contents

WHAT IS A MATERIAL?

What's the big idea?

Materials are what things are made of.
Some materials are natural and some are not.

Material world

1. Look at these pictures. Which of the following are materials?

Living things are not materials. Some materials were once part of a living thing. Wool, ivory and leather are examples of these. Some materials are made from minerals in rocks. These have never been alive.

Wood and paper are materials made from trees, which were once alive.
Iron was once part of rocks in the Earth.
Coal is fossilised wood, pressed between layers of rocks for millions of years.

2. List five other materials that were once part of a living thing.

Kitchen materials

Some building materials are manufactured or artificial. This means people have made them. Bricks, glass and plastics are artificial.

3. Look at the picture above of a kitchen. Decide which objects are made from artificial material and which are made from natural material. Don't forget the fabrics.

List the objects, what they are made from and then describe them.

Object	Material it is made from	Natural or artificial	My description
window	glass		The glass in the picture is clear. It is transparent and it may break easily.

Your challenge ...

Make your own card game. Work with a partner. On one card write the name of an animal or plant. On another card, write any materials that are produced from it. Record as many examples as you can think of. Shuffle the cards and play 'snap'.

MATERIAL WORDS

What's the big idea?

Each material has particular properties.
We choose materials for a purpose because of their properties.

What's the word?

Every material has specific properties. These allow us to recognise the material.

Here are some important properties.

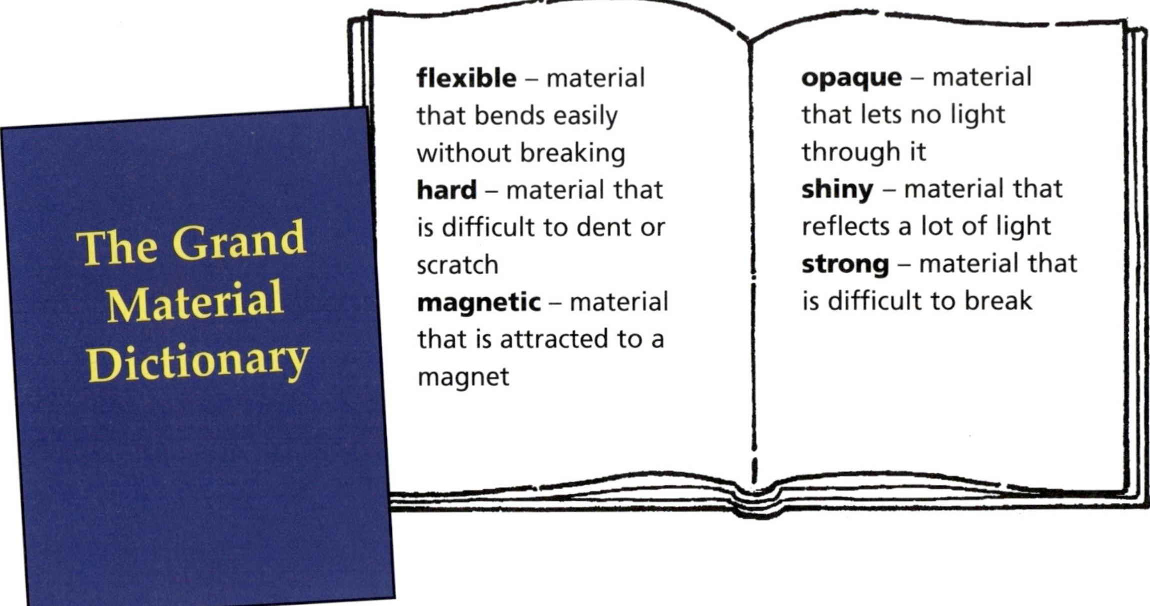

1. Each of the words in *The Grand Material Dictionary* has an opposite word. Can you find the opposite? Provide a definition for each word. Use the explanations shown above to help you.

2. Make your own scientific dictionary. Here are some more words to help you start.

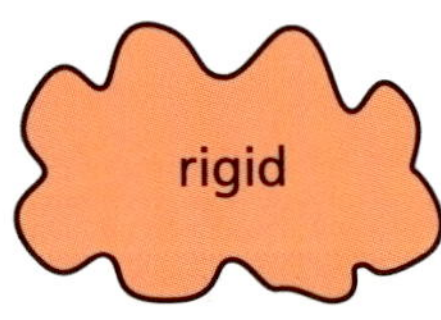

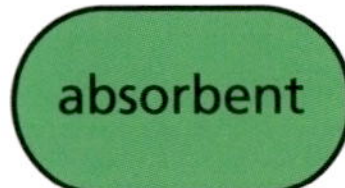

Strong or hard?

People find it difficult to explain the difference between hard and strong. Look at the picture of Rachel and Imran investigating materials.

3. Who is testing hardness and who is testing strength?
4. How can you tell?

Your challenge ...

Materials are chosen for some purposes because they are strong and rigid. The shape of an object can be important too. Roll a sheet of paper into a tube. Will it support a 1kg weight? Try different diameter tubes. Does the diameter matter?

Characteristics of Materials

KEEP DRY

What's the big idea?

Some materials let water pass through.
Waterproof materials do not let water through.

Waterproof

When it is raining we want to stay dry. The materials that raincoats, umbrellas and buildings are made from are **waterproof**. They do not let water through. Some materials are given a special treatment to make them waterproof.

Some tents need to be sprayed with waterproofing spray.

A waxed jacket has a wax coating to keep the rain out.

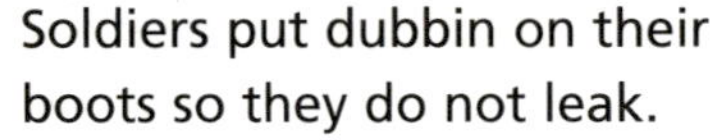
Soldiers put dubbin on their boots so they do not leak.

1. What other examples can you think of?

The Macintosh story

Charles Macintosh was a Scotsman who made a very important discovery.

1815, Clothes Dyeing Factory, Glasgow. Charles Macintosh had been using chemicals to clean his machines.

The chemicals we use to clean the machines can turn rubber into liquid.

This got Macintosh thinking.

Can I make a sheet of rubber as a waterproof layer?

This liquid rubber will stick to cloth. It will make the cloth waterproof!

By putting a layer of rubber between two sheets of cotton, Macintosh made a waterproof material.

Here is the first waterproof coat. I've called it the macintosh.

Charles Macintosh made things waterproof by taking cotton and adding a layer of rubber.

2. Investigate what you could add to cotton to make it waterproof. Here are some suggestions: Vaseline, PVA glue, wax crayon, polish.

Your challenge ...

Charles Macintosh was not liked by all doctors in the 1800s. They said that his macintosh was not healthy because it kept the sweat in. Today, you can buy jackets made of 'breathable' material which are waterproof. Find out who wears them and why. Can you find out how they work?

GET WET, STAY DRY

What's the big idea?

Some materials absorb water, which means that they take up water. Absorbent materials are useful.

Absorbing stuff

When water is taken up into a material, we say that the material is **absorbent**.
Absorbent is not the same as waterproof.

Tiled roof

The roof tiles on most houses are waterproof. They do not absorb water.

Thatched roof

Reed and straw thatches on old houses are continuously wet, but they do not let water through to the rooms below.

1. What useful properties do absorbent materials have and why are they useful?

Keeping baby dry

The outside of a disposable nappy is waterproof so that it does not leak. The inside is made to absorb liquid. The more liquid a nappy absorbs, the drier the baby's skin will be.

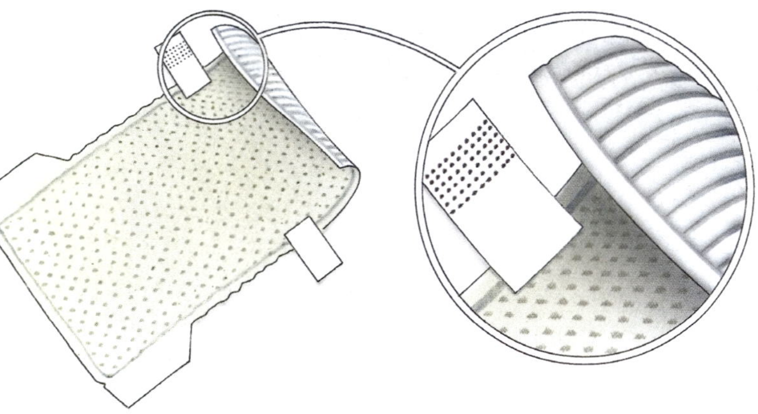

What do the makers say?

Advertisements tell us that some paper towels are very absorbent.

2. How could you test which type of paper towel was the best at absorbing water?

You need to pour some water on the paper towel and see how much it takes up.

3. How much water will you need to use? Why is the amount important?
4. How will you know how much water was absorbed?
5. Create a table and write a measurement in cubic centimetres to show how much liquid was absorbed by each type of paper towel.

Your challenge ...

Advertisements say that certain tissues are absorbent but also strong. Think about what the word strong means.
Why do tissues need to be strong?
Do they need to be strong when they are dry or when they are wet?
How would you investigate different types of tissue?

MATERIALS FOR THE JOB

What's the big idea?

We choose materials for a purpose because they have the right properties. Sometimes there may be more than one material with suitable properties.

Plane sense

The first aeroplanes were made by stretching fabric over a metal or wood frame. They were very light but not strong.

France, 1909

1. Why do you think the weight of the materials was more important than their strength?

By the 1940s, most aeroplanes were made from metal. Some parts were made from steel because it is very strong. Other parts were made from aluminium because it is lighter than steel.

2. Steel rusts easily. Why is this a problem for an aircraft?

Today aircraft are made from **steel**, **aluminium** and **composites**. Composites are mixtures of materials; fibreglass is an example. They are made light and strong. Modern composites are more expensive than steel or aluminium.

Handing in scrap metal for use in the war industry

A job to do

SITUATIONS VACANT

METAL FOR PLUMBING REQUIRED

Job for a metal that can be shaped into tubes and must not rust in a damp workplace.

JOB VACANT

Flexible at work and can be clear. Good as a ruler or an old bag.

CHRISTMAS HOLIDAY JOB

Shiny when polished, light metal but able to foil chickens when needed. Must not rust.

GOOD NAILS REQUIRED

Rigid or stiff and can be hard as nails. Can be found to be rusty at times.

ERASER WANTED

Always opaque and must never be clear. Good at cleaning up other people's mistakes. Needs to be flexible.

3. Which material should apply for each of these jobs? Choose from iron, rubber, polythene, copper and aluminium.

Your challenge ...

Write your own job descriptions for paper and glass.
Try to use at least two words from* The Grand Material Dictionary *(on page 6).

WHAT IS THE CONTRACTION?

What's the big idea?

Magnets can exert forces on each other without touching.

Pushes and pulls

Some toys use magnets and others use springs.

1. Which of the following toys contain a spring?

Magnets are special because they can push or pull things without touching them. Scientists say that magnets have a **magnetic force**.

Sometimes two magnets will push each other apart. We say they **repel** each other. Sometimes magnets pull together. We say they **attract** each other.

Investigation

There are many types of magnet. You may have magnets that have a red end and a blue end.

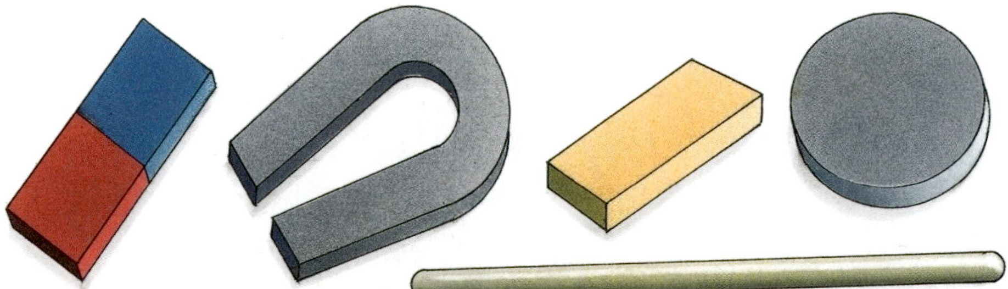

2. What happens If you put the same-coloured ends together?
3. What happens when the colours are different?

4. Craig recorded the following in his science book.

Use your magnets to check whether he is right.

Poles placed close	Result
red near red	repel
red near blue	attract
blue near red	attract
blue near blue	repel

Due north

William Gilbert was a doctor in England. In 1600, he published a book that described how the Earth behaved like a magnet. Most people call the red end of a magnet the **north-seeking pole** and the blue end the **south-seeking pole**. Scientists think that the Earth behaves like a magnet because it has an iron core.

Your challenge ...

Make up a rule that describes how the poles of a magnet always behave.
Why is the north pole of a magnet called the north pole?
Does this follow your rule?

MAGNETIC MATERIALS

What's the big idea?

Some metals are magnetic, but most are not.
Recycling materials is important to protect the Earth's resources.

Magnetic or not?

Magnets can attract each other and some materials that are not magnets.

1. Suzie decides her pipes must be made of plastic, because if they were made of metal they would stick to the magnet. Is she right? Explain your answer.

Your teacher will show you a set of materials. Predict:

2. Are all the metals in the set magnetic?
3. Are any of the other materials magnetic?
4. List the materials in a table. Record your prediction for each one. Then test your prediction with a magnet.

Object	My prediction	My result
string iron nail	not magnetic	not magnetic

Scientists try to write clear sentences that summarise their ideas.

5. Summarise what you have found out about materials that are magnetic and those that are not.

Magnetic materials

People often think that all metals are magnetic. They are wrong. Magnetic materials are usually made of iron or steel. Other magnetic metals include cobalt and nickel. Some objects are made of a mixture of metals called an **alloy**. If an alloy contains enough iron it will be magnetic.

Recycling

Magnets are used in lots of ways, such as sorting metals for recycling. Aluminium cans are often collected in recycling banks. Some cans contain iron or steel. These too can be recycled, but it is important not to mix them up with aluminium.

6. How could you find out whether a can contained iron or steel?

1. Every month a lorry comes to collect the bin full of cans.

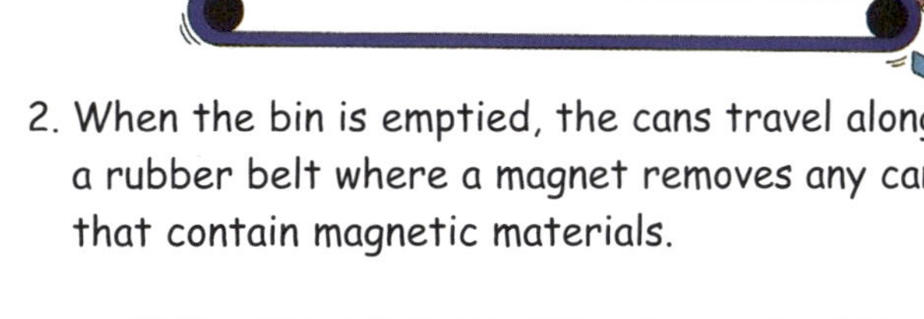

2. When the bin is emptied, the cans travel along a rubber belt where a magnet removes any cans that contain magnetic materials.

3. The aluminium cans are heated in a furnace where the aluminium becomes so hot that it melts.

4. The shiny liquid metal is collected at the bottom of the furnace and is put into moulds where it forms blocks of aluminium. The aluminium is then re-used.

An ingot made from 1.5 million used drink cans

Your challenge ...

Write a careful description of the changes to the material aluminium as it is recycled. Use the correct names for these changes. Which changes can be reversed?

MAGNETIC SHIELDING

What's the big idea?

Magnetic force can pass through some materials, but not others.
This is an idea that we can test scientifically.

Scientists ask questions

A strong magnetic force can sometimes cause problems.
Perhaps some materials can block a magnetic force.

1. Write this idea as a question that you can investigate.

Scientists make predictions

2. What sort of materials do you think will block a magnetic force?
3. What sort of materials will a magnetic force go through?
Write down your ideas.

Scientists test their ideas

4. How can you test your ideas?
5. How can you make your test fair?
6. What is the one thing you will change? What must you keep the same?
Write down your ideas.

These pictures show some ways different children tried this investigation.

7. Explain what will happen in each test.

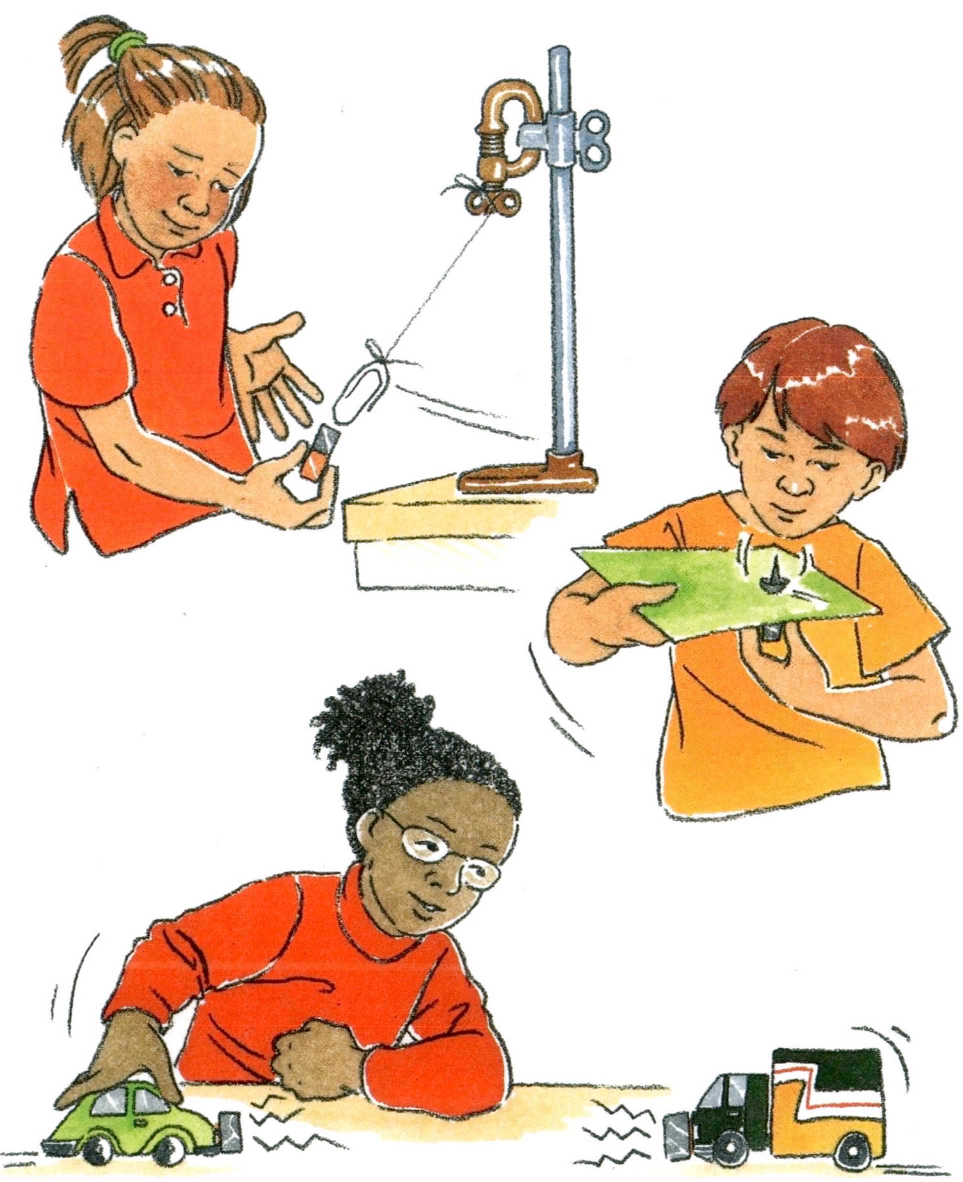

8. Now carry out your own investigation.
Talk to your teacher about what you are going to do.

Scientists keep records

Record your results in a table.

Name of object	Material of object	Did it block the magnetism?
wooden ruler	wood	yes

Your challenge ...

You have already found out that magnetic force goes through cardboard.
Does it matter how thick the cardboard is?
Test out your ideas.

SPRINGS

What's the big idea?

Some springs can be compressed (squashed) and some springs can be extended (stretched).
If you extend a spring, it pulls back.
If you compress a spring, it pushes back.

Push me, pull you

1. Look at the following pictures. Which springs are getting squashed?

When you sit on a bed, you push the springs with a downward push.

2. Which way does the spring push back?

When you stretch a chest expander, you pull it outwards.

3. Which way does the spring pull back?

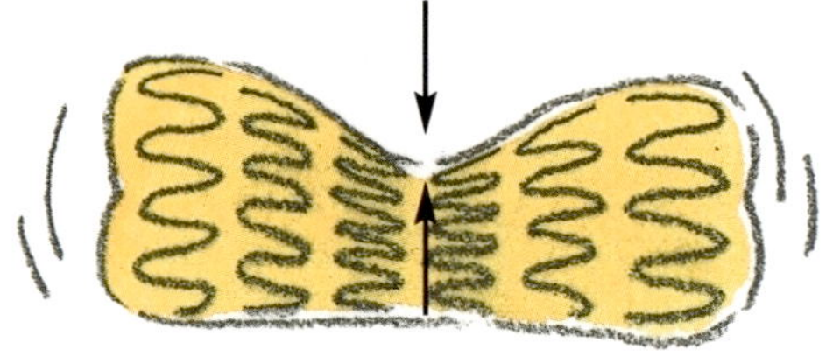

If you apply force to a spring in one direction, there will be a force back in the opposite direction. We can show the direction of forces using arrows.

A pull for a pull

Your teacher will give you some items that contain springs. Try squashing or stretching each item and think about what is happening to the spring.

4. If you pull the spring, which way does it pull back on you?
5. If you push the spring, which way does it push back on you?

6. Copy these pictures and draw arrows to show the direction of force of the spring. Which way is the spring pushing or pulling? Make your arrow go the same way.

Jack-in-the-Box pops up.

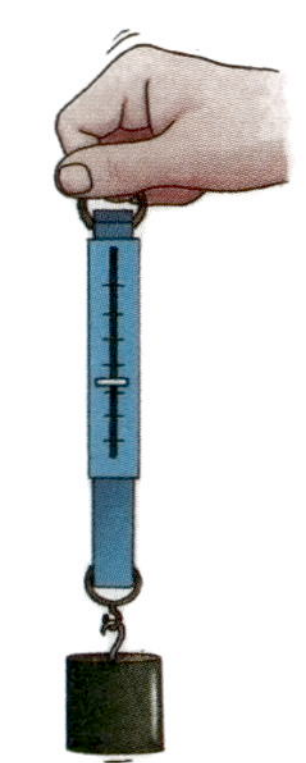

The forcemeter is stretched.

The toy frog is ready to jump.

Springs are elastic

Elastic means that once you stop extending or compressing a material, it goes back to its original size and shape.

We often think the word **elastic** is used to mean a material. We say our underwear is held up by elastic. If the material were not elastic we might have a problem!

7. Can you explain this joke?

Your challenge ...

How many elastic things do you think you could find in your bedroom?
Make a list or a collage to show your ideas.

STRETCHING PATTERNS

What's the big idea?

Rubber bands extend rather like a spring.
You can use a rubber band to apply a force to another object.

Band ideas

Rubber bands are elastic. Remember: the word **elastic** means that something goes back to its starting size and shape when you stop pulling or pushing it.

Jane is using a rubber band catapult to make a toy car move across the floor.

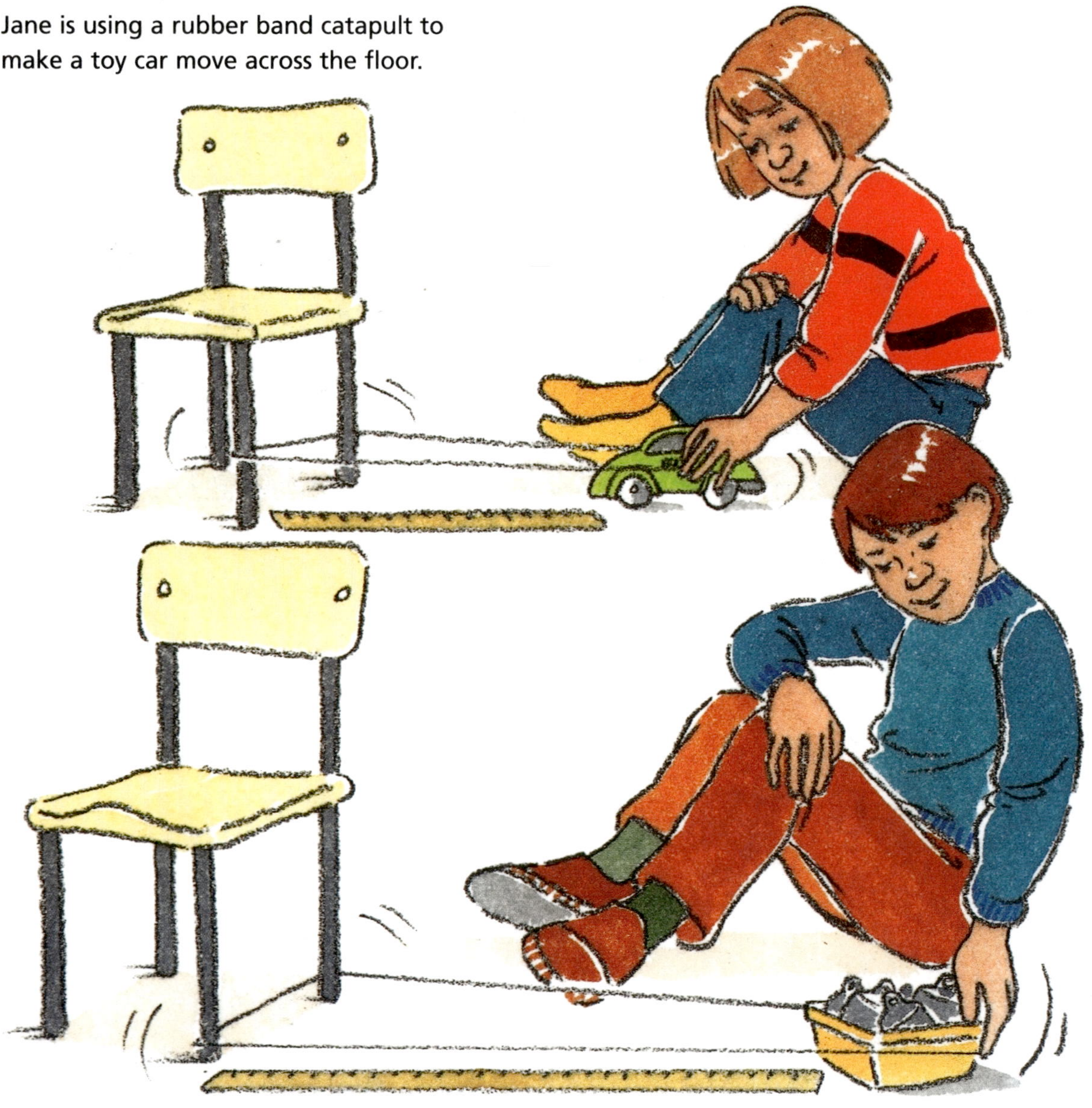

Peter is using his rubber band catapult to move a tub of weights in the same way.

Investigating catapults

Look at the catapults in the pictures.

1. **How could Jane make her car move further across the floor?**
2. **What would happen if she added another rubber band to her catapult?**
3. **How could Peter prevent the tub moving so far across the floor?**
4. **Could he do this without changing the position of the rubber band?**

Investigate either:

5. **How does the distance the rubber band is pulled back affect the distance the object travels?**

or

6. **How does the amount of weight affect how far it travels?**

7. **What do you predict will happen in your investigation?**
   Copy these sentences and fill in the missing words.

> The further back you pull the rubber band, the
>
> ____________________ the object will travel.
>
> The heavier the object is, the ____________________ it will travel.

8. **In which investigation must you pull the rubber band back the same distance every time?**

Think about the following before you design your fair test:

- the number of rubber bands you use
- the surface your car or tub moves on
- how far you pull the rubber bands back
- the weight of the object you are using.

Record your results in a table.

Your challenge ...

Show the results of your investigation as a graph. It will be easier to draw a graph if you refer to your table. You may be able to use a spreadsheet on a computer.

LET'S CLASSIFY

What's the big idea?

Living and non-living things can be grouped according to their features.
Some non-living things were once alive, others have never lived.

Dead or alive?

1. Look at this picture. How many living things can you identify? Write your own list and then compare it with a partner's list.
2. Find two things in the picture that:
   - are made of stone
   - were once alive.

Birds, animals, trees and grass are all **living**. Glass, metal and ceramics were **never alive**. They are made from natural materials. Things that are not alive are called **non-living**.

3. Which group would you put wood and paper into?
   Wood and paper both come from trees, which are living things.
4. Make a list of other materials that come from things that were once alive.

Scientific sorting

Scientists need ways of grouping in order to be able to understand different kinds of animals and plants. Scientists have to agree how to group (or classify) living things. They need to be sure that what one scientist defines as a bear is the same animal that another scientist calls a bear.

Polar bear

Brown bear

5. List at least five features that would help you recognise a bear.
6. How many different kinds of living thing did you see on your way to school?

To organise your bedroom you group clothes into one place, toys into another and books on a shelf. Scientists sort into groups too.

7. Your teacher will provide you with pictures for sorting. Consider the following questions. What is this made of? Is it living? Was it once alive? Was it part of something that was once alive?

8. Now, sort the pictures into:
   - Living and non-living
   - Animals and plants.

   Record your work in a clear way. This might be a table or a list.

Your challenge ...

Find out why spiders are not classified as insects.

Teeth and Eating

FOOD TO SURVIVE

What's the big idea?

Animals need particular conditions and particular types of food to survive and be healthy. Our 'diet' is all the things we usually eat.

Who am I?

1. Complete these riddles.

I eat flakes and pellets I can pick food from the gravel I eat less than most animals in the pet shop I am a _____________ .	My favourite foods are cucumber and lettuce I have a cuttlefish to keep my shell strong I move on my muscle-like foot I am a _____________ .

What do I eat?

All animals need food to stay alive, to grow and be active.

We call animals that eat just plants **herbivores**.

We call animals that eat just meat **carnivores**.

We call animals that eat both plants and meat **omnivores**.

2. What do we call a human who only eats plants?

An animal survey

3. Carry out a survey in your school of the pets that people keep. You will need to think of questions to ask. A sample questionnaire is provided below. Use one for each pet.

Do you have any pets?

yes ☐ no ☐

What kind of pets do you have?

cat ☐ dog ☐ fish ☐ bird ☐

rabbit ☐ reptile ☐ other (name) ☐

How many do you have?

1 ☐ 2 ☐ 3 ☐ more than 3 ☐

Where does each pet live?

in the house ☐ in a pond ☐ in a cage ☐ other ☐

What does each pet eat?

seed ☐ grass ☐ mixed diet ☐ tinned food ☐

specialist food ☐ other ☐

4. Produce a bar chart to show the number of each type of pet in your school. The groups on the *x*-axis will be the same as the groups on your survey sheet.

Your challenge ...

Think of an animal. It may be a pet or a wild animal. Write a riddle for that animal but do not tell anyone what the animal is. Who can solve your riddle first?
Vets are animal doctors. The word 'vet' is an abbreviation for what word? What subjects do you have to study before you could begin to train as a vet?

A SQUARE MEAL

What's the big idea?

There are many types of food that humans can eat. We need a balance of the main types.

Food groups

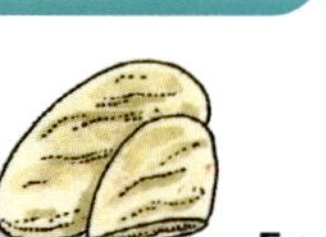

Foods for activity are STARCHES and SUGARS.

Foods for activity, for storage and for keeping skin supple are FATS.

Foods for growth.

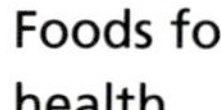

Foods for health.

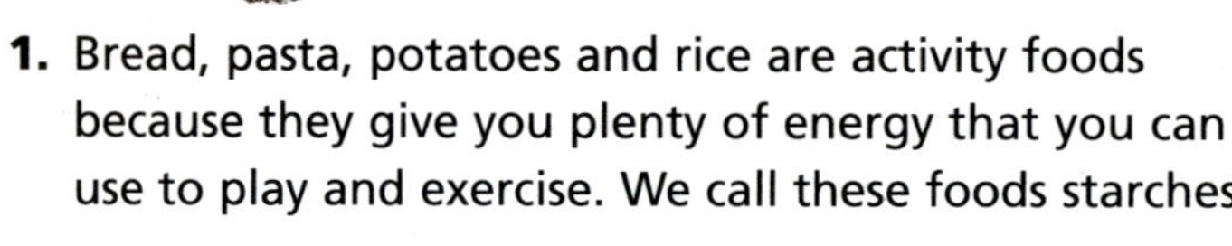
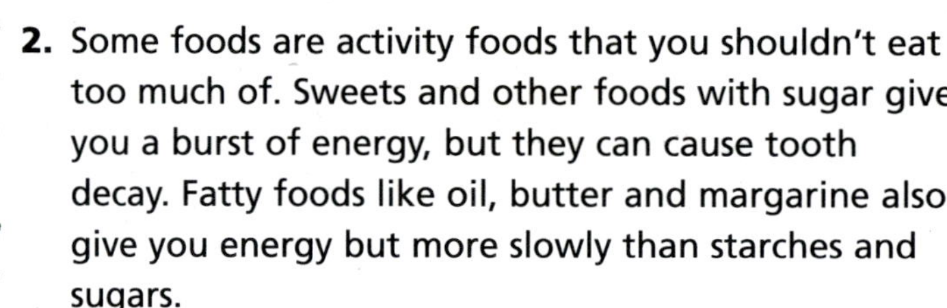
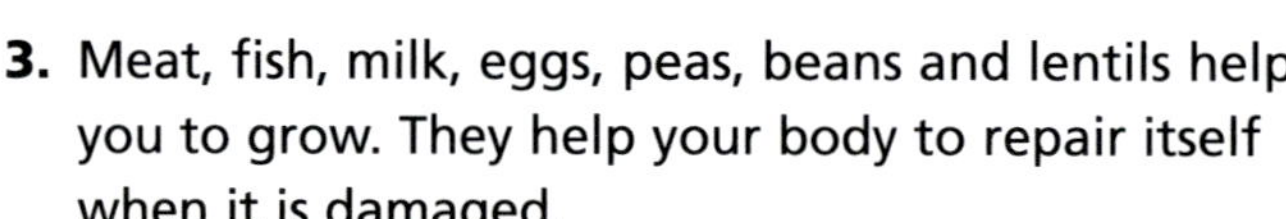
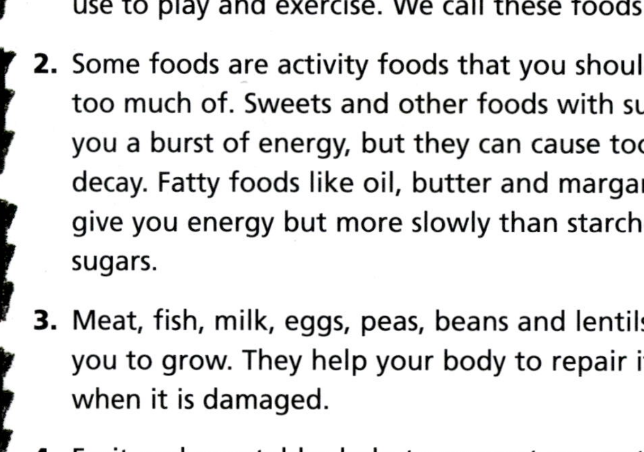

1. Bread, pasta, potatoes and rice are activity foods because they give you plenty of energy that you can use to play and exercise. We call these foods starches.
2. Some foods are activity foods that you shouldn't eat too much of. Sweets and other foods with sugar give you a burst of energy, but they can cause tooth decay. Fatty foods like oil, butter and margarine also give you energy but more slowly than starches and sugars.
3. Meat, fish, milk, eggs, peas, beans and lentils help you to grow. They help your body to repair itself when it is damaged.
4. Fruit and vegetables help to prevent you getting ill.

1. When did you last eat something from the  group?

2. What did you last eat from the  group?

A square meal

A balanced meal has food from each of the four groups.

3. Why do you think some people call this a square meal?

The meals below are not square meals.

4. What would you add to each meal to make it a square meal?

Your challenge ...

Try to design a school meal. Think about what it should contain. It should not cost more than £2.00. Is it a square meal?

Teeth and Eating

OUR TEETH

What's the big idea?

Humans have three different types of teeth. Each type has a different function.
Animals have teeth suited to the food they eat.

You and your teeth

Teeth can do different types of job. Scientists call this their **function**. The shape of a tooth depends on its function. The teeth of an elephant are quite different from either human or shark teeth.

Lower teeth of a shark

Elephant molar teeth

Your teeth mash food so that it is easy to swallow. You begin to digest your food in your mouth.

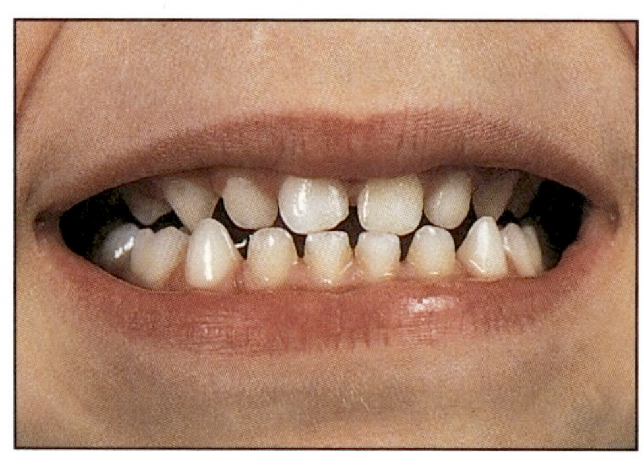

By the time you were four years old you probably had about twenty teeth. These are called **milk teeth**. They are not permanent teeth.

At the age of six or seven years old, permanent new teeth start to grow through your gums. The new teeth slowly push the milk teeth out. This gives the new teeth space to grow.

1. How many of your own teeth are permanent teeth?

There are thirty-two teeth in a full set of adult teeth. You may not get all your adult teeth until you are over twenty years old. If you lose an adult tooth, a new one does not grow.

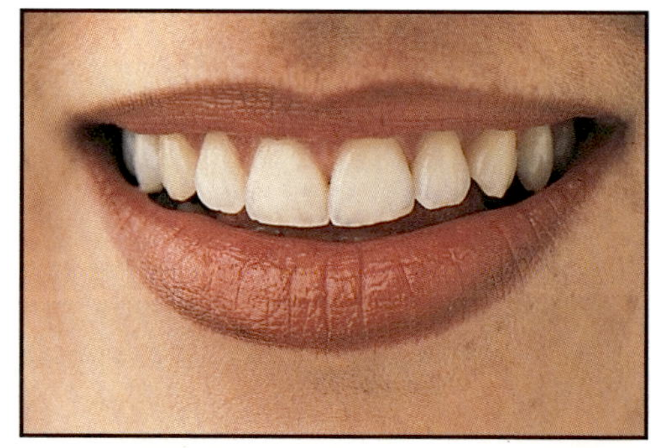

In your upper and lower jaw, there are three types of teeth. Each type has a different function.

Incisors are at the front of the mouth. They cut food like a chisel.

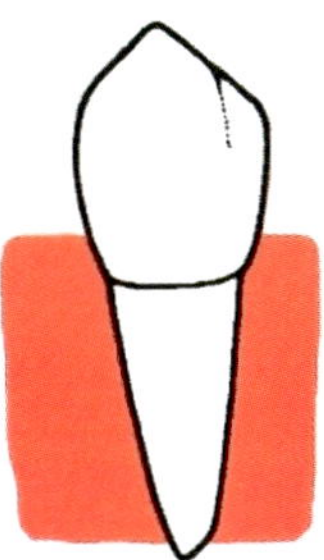

Canines are the sharp pointed teeth next to the incisors. They tear and hold food.

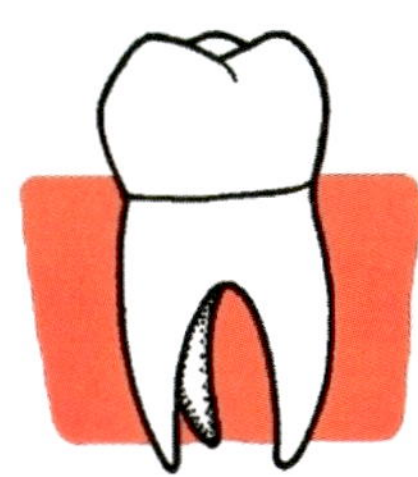

Molars are the flat wide teeth at the back of the mouth. They grind food.

Spot the teeth

The skull is the part of the skeleton that holds the teeth.
The pictures below show the skulls of a tiger, a deer and a human.

2. Can you identify which is which?

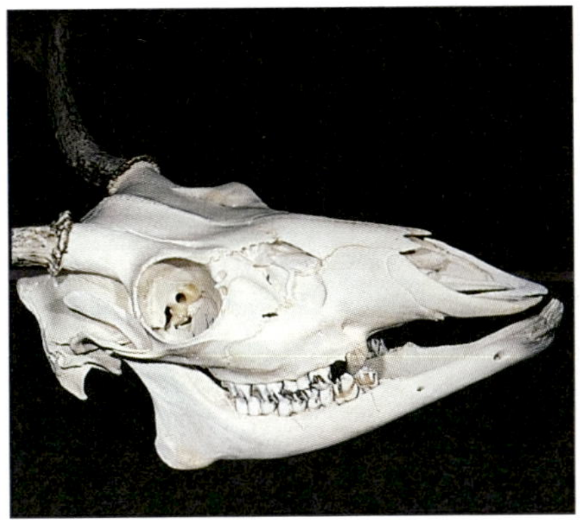

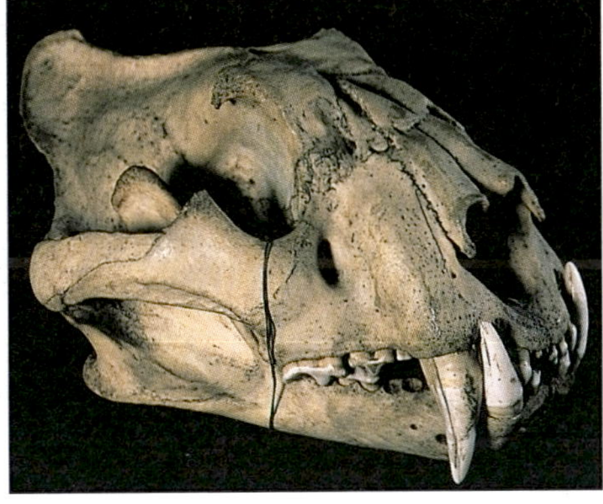

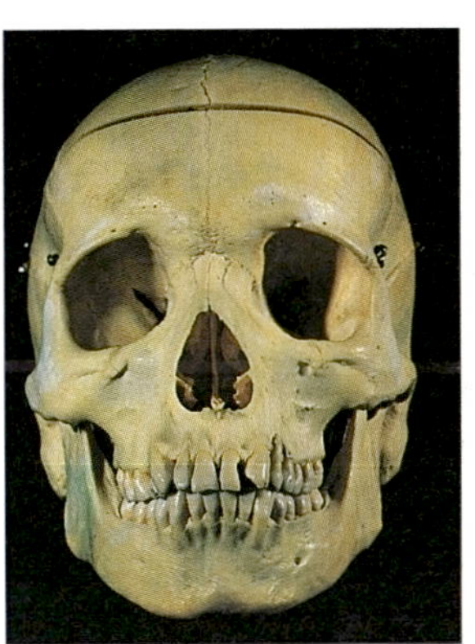

Carnivores eat meat. They need to hold and tear food.
A herbivore only eats plants. It doesn't hold its food down or tear it.
Herbivores grind and chew the plants. The smaller pieces are easier to digest.

3. What are the differences between the diet of a tiger and the diet of a deer?
4. Which is a herbivore and which is a carnivore?
5. What are the differences between the teeth in the two skulls?
6. Why do you think there are differences?
7. Humans are omnivores. How are our teeth similar to those of deer and tigers? How are they different?

Your challenge ...

Teeth are not made of the same material all the way through. Use reference material to find out what is inside a tooth and what materials teeth are made of.
How are the properties of these materials useful?

I WISH I'D LOOKED AFTER MY TEETH

What's the big idea?

Sugary food leads to plaque forming on your teeth.
Bacteria live on the plaque and produce acid, which damages teeth.

A sticky problem

1. What should you do to look after your teeth?

Brushing with toothpaste twice a day removes **plaque**. Plaque is a mixture of food particles and tiny organisms called **bacteria**. The bacteria make **acid** from the plaque. Acid rots your teeth. We call this **tooth decay**.

A decaying tooth

A sticky layer of plaque starts to form on the teeth.

↓

Bacteria grow and produce acid.

↓

Acid causes the tooth to rot.

gum

2. Why do you think it is important to brush your teeth before you go to bed?

Regular visits to the dentist help the dentist to spot the first signs of plaque and decay.

3. What does the dentist do during an inspection?

The dentist will check that there is no decay. If there are holes in your teeth, the dentist will fill them to prevent more damage. Sometimes hard **tartar** builds up on your teeth. This can harm your gums. The dentist will scrape the tartar away. Gum disease can make you lose your permanent teeth.

Mr Gum has not been to the dentist for five years!

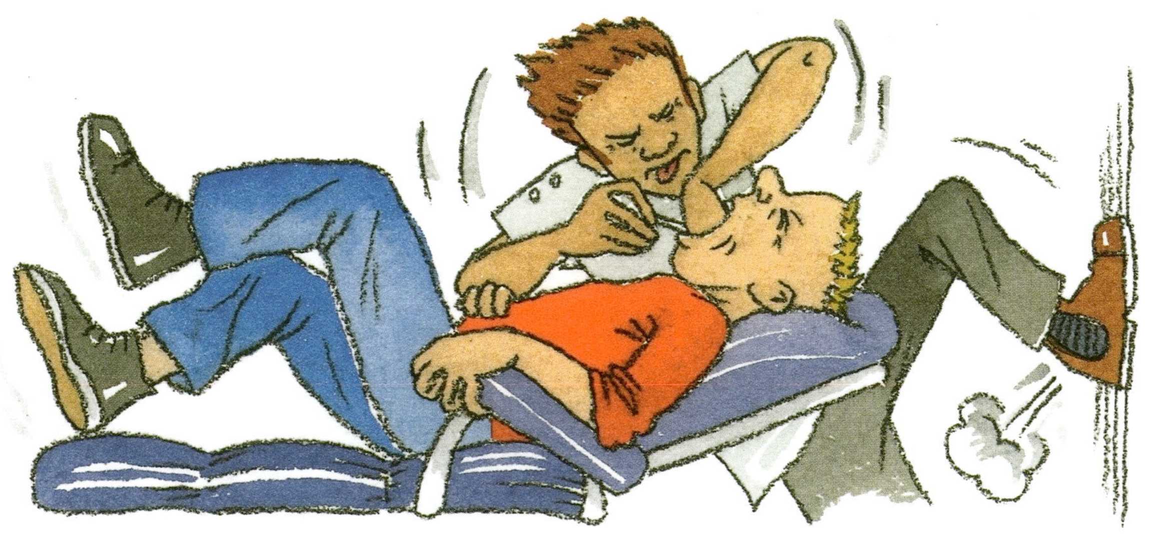

A four-point plan for healthy teeth

1. Brush your teeth twice a day.
2. Use fluoride toothpaste to make your teeth stronger.
3. Eat less sugary food.
4. Go to the dentist twice a year.

You can buy tablets to show you where the plaque is in your mouth. They are called **disclosing tablets**. They help you to see where the teeth need brushing to remove food particles and plaque.

Your challenge ...

Design a tooth-shaped poster to encourage others to look after their teeth. Use scientific words but make the message clear and easy to remember.

ROCK SPOTTING

What's the big idea?

There are three main types of rock. These were formed in different ways.

What are rocks?

Rocks are what the planet Earth is made from.

Some rocks are made of tiny grains all joined together.

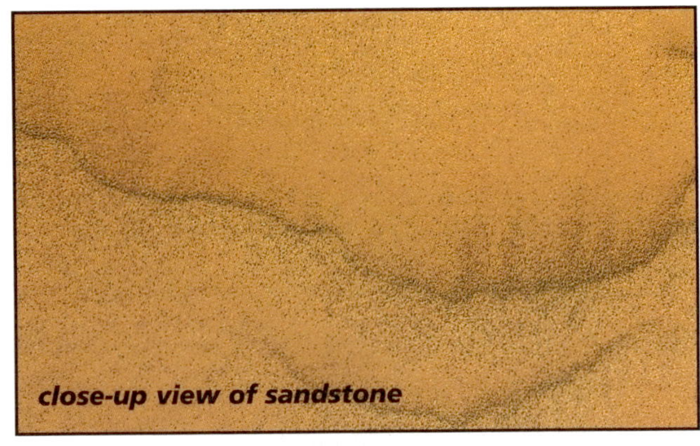
close-up view of sandstone

Some rocks sparkle, as if they have glitter in them. The shiny parts are crystals. Sometimes these crystals are big.

close-up view of pink granite

close-up view of basalt

close-up view of slate

Some rocks are shiny like glass and others are pushed into very flat layers.

Here are the names of some different rocks: granite, basalt, slate, sandstone, limestone, marble.

How to use a hand lens

- You must learn to use a hand lens correctly or you will not see anything clearly.
- Put the rock sample 20–30cm away from your eye.
- Put the hand lens between your eye and the rock.
- Move the lens, not your head, to see the make-up of the rock more clearly.

Rock records

A **database** is a way of storing information so that someone else can find things out quickly. Databases can be created using a computer program, or on paper in the form of a table.

1. Conduct your own investigation. Use a hand lens to look at different rocks and record exactly what you see. Your results should be recorded in a database.

When describing rocks, use adjectives for colour, shape and texture.

Record:
- the colours of the rock
- whether there are crystals
- whether there are tiny bits joined together, like a clump of sand
- whether there are flat layers.

You need to:
- decide which rocks to include in your database
- choose some facts to find out about each one
- write down your facts in a table.

2. Use encyclopaedias, books and CD-ROMs to find out how each of the rocks formed.

Rock Database			
Name of rock	**Colours in the rock**	**Does it have crystals?**	**How did it form?**
basalt	black and grey	yes	

Your challenge ...

In a small group, play 'Guess which rock'.
One person should refer to a rock database and silently choose a rock. The other members of the group have to try to guess which rock has been chosen. Each person can ask one question. Only 'yes' or 'no' answers can be given. When someone thinks they know the rock, they raise their hand. The first person to guess correctly scores a point.

INVESTIGATING ROCKS

What's the big idea?

Different rocks have different properties.
Hardness and permeability are important properties of rock.

Hard rock

The first tools were made from pieces of wood, bone or stones. Later, people used a type of stone called **flint**. Flint is very hard, so it did not dent or wear away easily. It could be used for shaping wood.

1. Think of three other uses for flint.

Limestone is a softer rock than flint. The Egyptians used it thousands of years ago in building the pyramids. Limestone has been used to build many cathedrals and statues. Limestone is strong and easy to shape.

2. What has happened to a lot of limestone statues now?

Lion killing horse statue

Sphinx

3. Think of three other uses for limestone.

A scale of hardness

Scientists give numbers to the hardness of a rock.

1. Rock can easily be scratched by a fingernail.
2. Rock can be scratched by a fingernail.
3. Rock can be scratched with a copper penny.
4. Rock can be scratched with an iron nail.
5. Rock can be scratched with difficulty using an iron nail.
6. Rock can be scratched with a steel file.
7. Rock can be scratched by the edge of flint.

Letting water in

Slate is used for roofs because it does not absorb water and it is easy to split into thin, flat sheets. Limestone absorbs water and is not good for making roofs. We describe rocks that absorb water as **permeable**.

4. Think of three uses for permeable rock.

Which property?

5. Look at the pictures. Which tests are for hardness and which are testing if the rocks are permeable?

6. Plan a fair test for one of these properties.

In your plan you must:

- write an instruction to state what you will do
- list all the things you will keep the same to make your test fair
- think of anything you need to do to keep yourself safe and to work safely.

Your challenge ...

Find out why some rocks that were formed from lava out of volcanoes contain lots of holes. Some of these rocks are so light they float on water!

WHY ARE ROCKS SO DIFFERENT?

What's the big idea?

Different types of rock look very different from each other. This is because of the way they were formed.

Rocks close-up

You are going to look closely at rocks. You will be on a quest to find:

- crystals
- grains
- layers or shininess.

Looking for crystals

Crystals have special regular shapes and are often some of the oldest rocks on Earth.

Basalt – contains tiny particles that catch the light.

Granite – contains mainly large crystals.

Millions of years ago, many rocks on our planet were so hot that they were liquid (molten). As they cooled, crystals formed inside them. Rocks that cooled quickly have tiny crystals. They glitter. Rocks that cooled slowly have bigger crystals. These rocks are called **igneous rocks**.

1. **Look up the word igneous and write a definition in your own words.**
2. **Why do you think these rocks were given this name?**
3. **Which rock cooled more quickly, basalt or granite?**

Looking for grains

Some rocks look like grains of sand joined together.
Sometimes the grains are big, sometimes they are much smaller.

Conglomerate – looks like bits of stone stuck together.

Sandstone – looks like grains of sand stuck together.

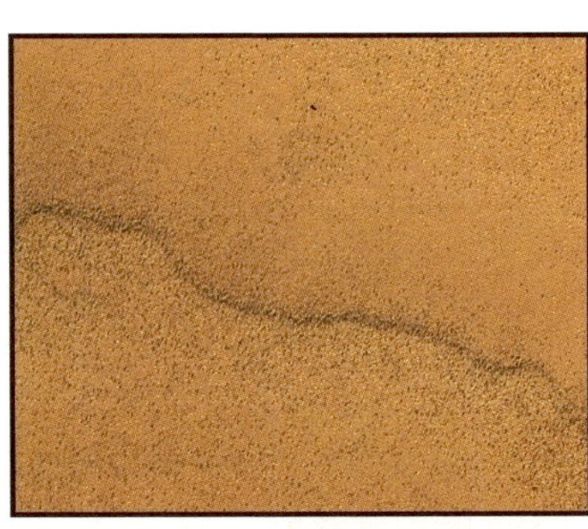

These rocks were often formed under the sea. The weight of the water forced the pieces together to form a new rock. These are called **sedimentary rocks**, which sometimes contain fossils.

Looking for rocks

There is a third group of rocks, which were formed in a different way. They are called **metamorphic rocks**. When rocks are deep under the surface, the weight of rock above them can squash them into layers. Other rocks look almost as shiny as glass because where they are formed, deep underground, is very hot.

Slate – looks as if it has been squashed into layers.

Marble – looks glassy and streaked.

Riddles

4. Complete the following riddles with the name of a type of rock.

I have lots of crystals of different colours
My crystals are big and I came from molten rock
I'm very hard and used for buildings and pavements
I am a rock called ____________________

I was once made of tiny parts but now I'm glassy
I get very shiny when I'm polished
I was formed with very great heat and pressure
I am a rock called ____________________

I formed under the sea from settling silt and mud
I have got shells and fossils inside me too
I look like sand and am light in colour
I am a rock called ____________________

5. Write your own riddles for a partner to solve.

Your challenge ...

Imagine that you are an igneous, sedimentary or metamorphic rock. Write a diary or a comic strip explaining what has happened to you over the many years it took you to form.

UNDER OUR FEET

What's the big idea?

There are several different types of soil.
They contain different amounts of sand, clay and material that was once alive.

Under your feet

Under Ground

In the deep kingdom under ground
There is no light and little sound.

Down below the earth's green floor
The rabbit and the mole explore.

The quarrying ants run to and fro
To make their populous empires grow.

Do they, as I pass overhead,
Stop in their work to hear my tread?

Some creatures sleep and do not toil,
Secure and warm beneath the soil.

Sometimes a fork or spade intrudes
Upon their earthly solitudes.

Downward the branching tree-roots spread
Into the country of the dead.

Deep down, the buried rocks and stones
Are like the earth's gigantic bones.

In the dark kingdom under ground
How many marvellous things are found!

James Reeves

What is soil?

Perhaps you think that all soil is the same. Not so!

Soils are mixtures. Some parts are the remains of living things, both plants and animals. This part of soil is called **humus**. Most of the soil is made of tiny bits of worn-down rock. The rest is water and dissolved minerals.

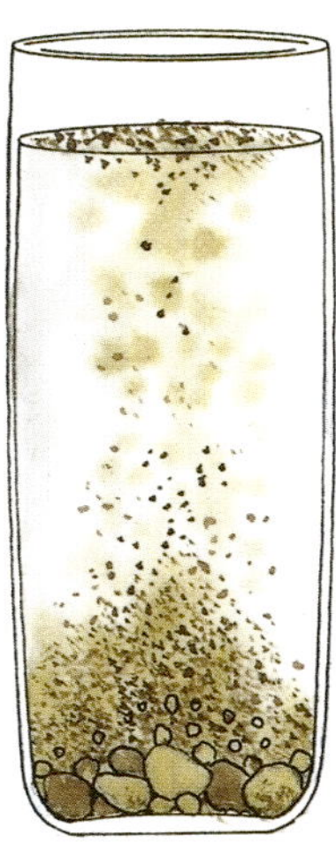

If you put a mixed soil into water and shake it, humus will float on top and gravel will sink to the bottom.

1. Why is the humus on top of the water?
2. Why are the largest particles at the bottom?

Different kinds of soil are found in different places. The type of soil depends on the type of rock from which it is made. Most soils are one of three types.

Clay soil is made of tiny particles that clump together. They are too small to be seen.

Silt is made of larger particles. It looks like powder.

Sand soil has grains the same size as sand. Its particles are larger than silt.

Separating soils

Soils can be separated using sieves to form samples in which the particles are of similar size. Sieves can have gaps of different sizes.

3. If you had a selection of sieves, which should you use first? Why?

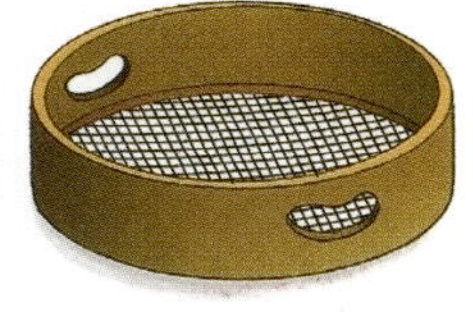

These samples have been separated in this way.

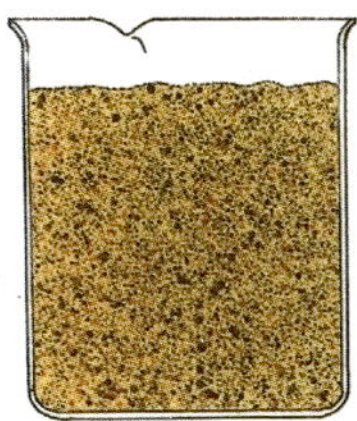

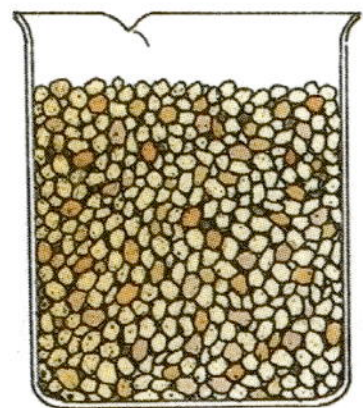

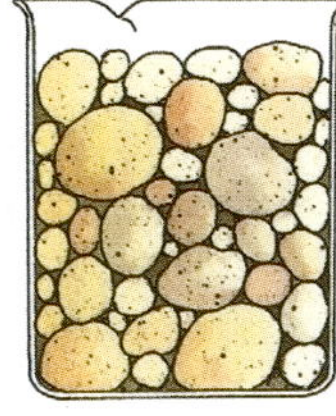

4. Which sample will have the biggest gaps?
5. Which sample will hold the most water?
6. Can you see a pattern?

Your challenge ...

Plants need water, but there is a limit to how much they can use. Too much water can damage plants, so soils through which the water can drain are usually good for plants.
Which do you think will drain most quickly: silt, clay or sandy soil? Why?
Plan a fair test to investigate how quickly water drains through these different types of soil.

GOING UNDERGROUND

What's the big idea?

Earthworms are good for the soil because they make air passages.

Darwin and the earthworms

Charles Darwin was a famous scientist. Some of his investigations were about earthworms.

Earthworm

One experiment took place in a field. No one, except Darwin and his assistants, could enter the field. He covered a part of the field with small rocks and pebbles.

Over the following years, the number of stones on the surface grew less. After thirty years, Darwin returned to find out what had happened to the stones.

He discovered the stones buried below the surface.

1. Think of two different explanations for what happened to the stones.
   Remember: nobody could get into the field.

Darwin's idea

Earthworms feed on plant material in the soil. The soil passes through their gut. This makes **worm casts**, which are very fine soil.

Close-up of worm casts

As they push their way through the soil, earthworms make air passages. They also break up the soil and turn it over.

2. How does this improve the soil?

3. What will eventually happen to heavy stones on the surface?

Darwin concluded that the stones sank into the ground because of what the worms were doing.

Farmers and gardeners need soil to drain, so that air and water can get to the roots of plants.

4. How do you think earthworms can help?

Your challenge ...

Do you think worms can hear? Explain your answer.

Charles Darwin investigated whether worms responded to sound. He put some worms in soil on top of his piano. He played different notes and found that low notes made the worms burrow under the soil. Why do you think they did this?

Helping Plants Grow Well

PLANT PARTS

What's the big idea?

Plants have parts that do different jobs.
Parts of some plants can be eaten for food.

Different parts

Here are some important parts of a daffodil and a strawberry plant.

LEAVES
Green leaves make new materials for growth from water and carbon dioxide in the air.

STEM
Carries water and nutrients from the roots to the leaves. Carries materials made in the leaves to other parts of the plant.

FRUIT
Develops from parts of the flower. It is a seed case. It protects the developing seeds.

FLOWER
Contains the parts that produce new seeds. Brightly coloured petals attract insects.

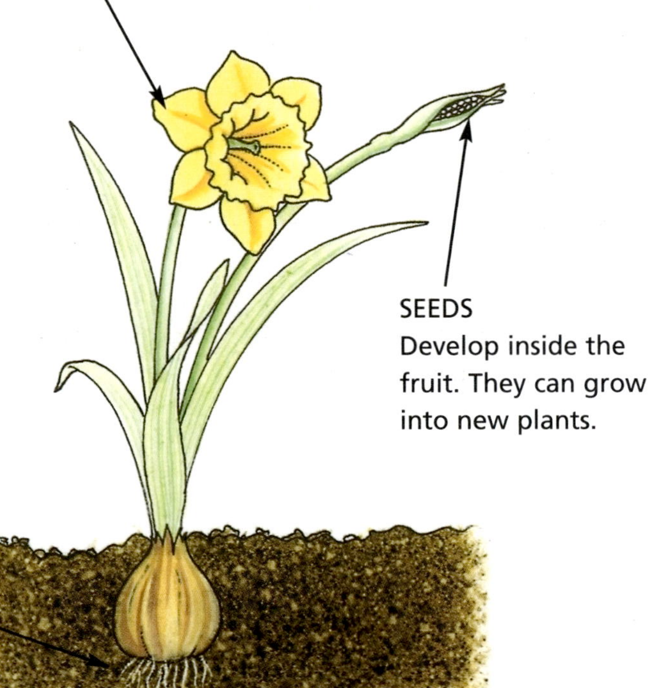

SEEDS
Develop inside the fruit. They can grow into new plants.

ROOTS
Anchor a plant in the soil. They take in water and mineral nutrients.

Looking at roots

A ship has an anchor that can hold the ship in one place.
A plant has a root to anchor it in the soil.

Water and mineral nutrients that a plant needs are in the soil. They enter the plant through its roots.

Some plants have roots with many fine branches. These are **fibrous roots**.
Other plants have one main root that holds the plant firmly in the ground. This is a **tap root**.

When you look closely at a root there are many tiny root hairs. These allow the plant to absorb more water. The plant needs water to go all around it. Tubes inside the stem help to carry the water to the leaves and flowers.

1. **Why do the leaves need water to reach them?**

Your challenge ...

On a large sheet of paper, design a 'perfect' plant for a particular habitat. Remember to include the roots. Think about the size and shape of the leaves and petals. You may choose any colours for the plant parts.

FOOD FOR ANIMALS

What's the big idea?

Plants are grown as food crops for humans and for farm animals.
We eat different parts of different plants.

Plants as food

Humans need to eat a variety of foods to stay healthy. Plants provide us with important types of food.

1. What plants are being harvested?

2. Which parts of the plant will people eat?

Here are some more examples.

We eat the leaves of lettuce.
We eat the fruits of tomatoes.
We eat the flowers of broccoli.
We eat the stems of rhubarb.
We eat the seeds of broad beans.
We eat the roots of turnips.

3. Think of some more examples for each part of a plant.

Fruit and seeds

A plant is a living thing. It can reproduce (make new plants). Flowering plants do this by making seeds.

The fruit of a plant is the part where the seeds develop. The fruit is a seed case. Not all fruits are sweet and juicy.

Bean pods and tomatoes are classed as fruit because they contain seeds.

Your challenge ...

Which of the following do you think contain seeds?
Which part of the plant do the others come from?

- ***aubergine***
- ***banana***
- ***celery***
- ***mango***
- ***melon***
- ***okra***
- ***orange***
- ***star fruit***
- ***turnip***
- ***yam***

Helping Plants Grow Well

PLANTS GROW

What's the big idea?

All living things grow. The growth of plants can be measured with different instruments.

Getting bigger

Living things grow until they are adult. Not every plant grows to the same height.

Some trees grow for hundreds of years. There are more than one hundred trees in the United Kingdom that are over one thousand years old.

1. How could you measure a plant?

2. What different measurements could you make?

Think about what is meant by growth. When you grow, you do not just get taller.

Growing rings

Trees are some of the largest plants on Earth and they grow all the way through their life. Each year in the British Isles a tree trunk gets slightly larger as a new layer of wood grows. This means as an oak tree gets older, its girth increases.

When a tree is cut down with a saw, you can see growth rings. These show how much the tree grew each year. There is one ring for each year.

3. Look at this drawing. How old was this tree when it was cut down?

Scientists use tree rings in old pieces of timber to discover which summers were dry and which were wet hundreds of years ago.

4. How do you think they can tell which growth rings were made in wetter years?

Measuring a tree

It is not easy to measure the size of a tree using a ruler!

5. How could you measure how wide a tree is?

6. How could you measure the distance round a tree?

Measuring the height of trees (or tall buildings) can be great fun. You will need a long tape measure and a clinometer.

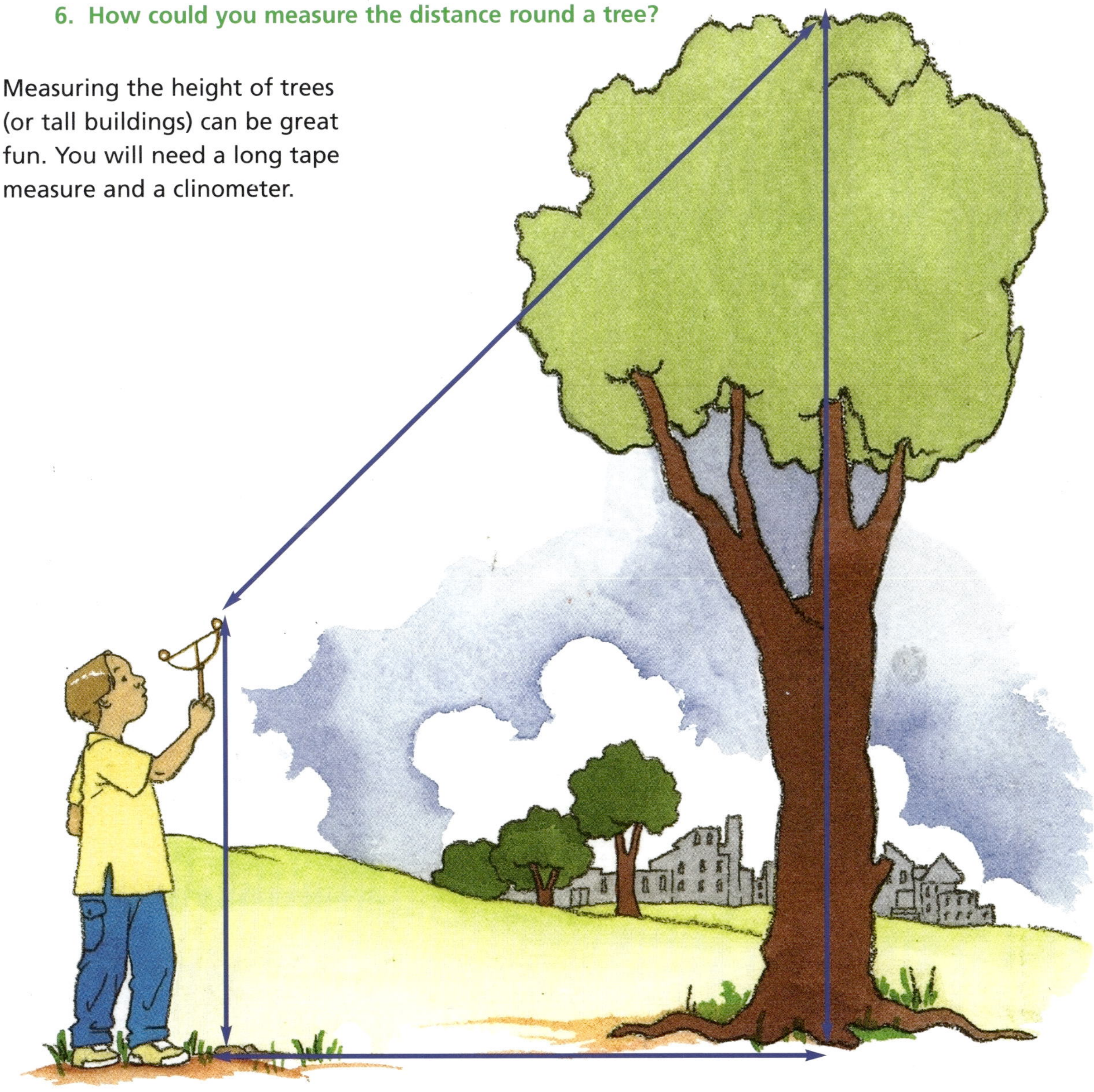

Distance to tree + height of user = height of tree.

Your challenge ...

Think of another way that you could measure the height of a tree. (You cannot reach the top of the tree, so you cannot use a tape measure.)
Hint: one way will only work on a sunny day!

NEW PLANTS FOR OLD

What's the big idea?

Plants need light and the right amount of water and heat to grow well.
Plants should not be given too much water.

Keeping plants healthy

Plants need the right sort of care to stay healthy.

1. **Look at these plants. They do not all look healthy. Can you think of some reasons why?**

A class of children decided to put a geranium plant in different places.

Plant 1 – in a cupboard, in the classroom, normal watering.
Plant 2 – in the well-lit classroom, no water.
Plant 3 – in the well-lit classroom, watered regularly.
Plant 4 – near the radiator and windowsill, normal watering.
Plant 5 – in a container of water with all soil washed away from the roots.

2. Which plant will be the healthiest? Why?

3. What does every plant need to stay healthy?

Investigating temperature

Scientists think of explanations for why things happen. Then they collect evidence to test their ideas. Here is one idea that scientists have tested and found to be true: plants need the right temperature to grow well.

4. What sort of evidence would you need to test this for yourself?

Scientists also have to make their tests fair. Here is a test that some children did. They wanted to find out if plants grow better when they are kept warm.

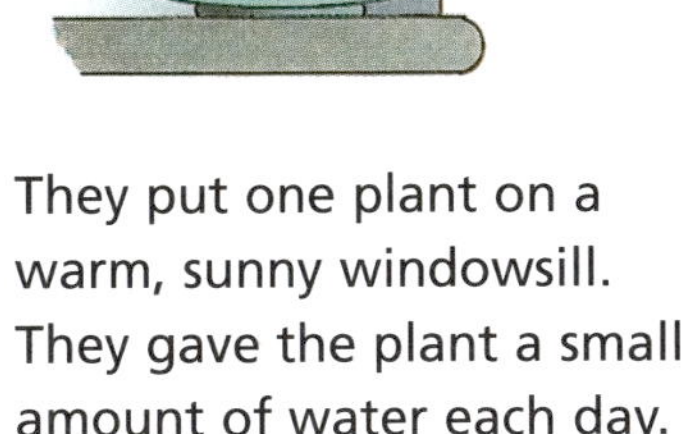

They put one plant on a warm, sunny windowsill. They gave the plant a small amount of water each day.

They put an identical plant in the fridge. They watered the second plant in the same way as the first.

They observed both plants each day.

5. Explain why this is not a fair test. Think about which things are the same for both plants and which are different.

Your challenge ...

How could you test the idea that plants grow better when they are kept warm? Plan an investigation.

HELPING PLANTS GROW WELL

What's the big idea?

Plants need water, air and light to make the new materials that they need for growth. Plants turn towards the light and roots grow towards water.

Plants on the move

Plants are living things. All living things can move.

1. **How have these plants moved?**
2. **Can you explain why?**

A growing plant needs light as well as heat, water and nutrients.
Roots tend to grow down, where they will find water and mineral nutrients. If the water is not straight below, the roots can change direction to where there is more water.
Stems and leaves need light. They grow away from the centre of the Earth.

Which way is up?

You have seen that plant roots grow down and stems grow up.

3. Does this mean that the seed has to be the right way up when it is planted? Investigate this question.

You may have planted bean seeds and seen how the roots grow down and the shoot grows up.

4. What will happen if you plant a seed sideways?
   Predict what will happen and make a drawing of it.
   Draw how you think the root will grow.
   Draw how you think the shoot will grow.
   Explain why you think this will happen.

Your challenge ...

Scientists have special names for the different ways that plants move. Here are some of them: phototropism, geotropism, hydrotropism.
Find out what these words mean and what 'photo', 'geo' and 'hydro' mean.

Light and Shadows

WHAT IS LIGHT?

What's the big idea?

Objects that give out their own light are light sources.

Lights

Examples of light sources are:
the Sun, the stars, fires and flames, electric light bulbs and candles.

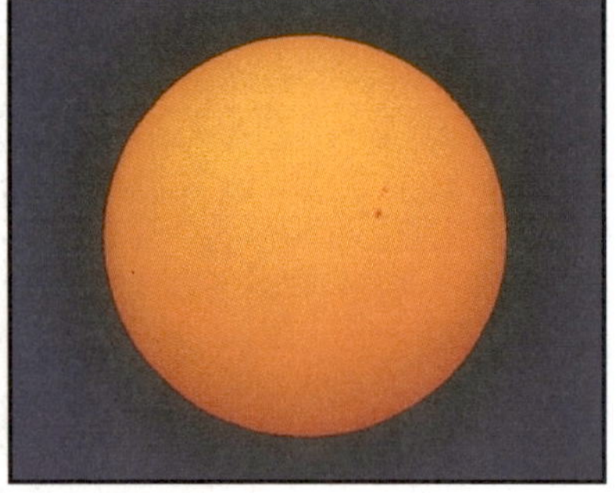

Imagine there were no lights in the world. We would not be able to see anything. Face a window or light source and close your eyes.

1. Can you see anything? What can you see?

Now cover your eyes with your hands.

2. Can you see anything now?

If we want to see we must have a source of light. Light sources allow us to see in a dark room.

Think about it

Light travels from a light source. A light source is something that gives out its own light.

Here is one pupil's list of light sources.
Only some of them are correct.

3. **Which ones are not light sources? Explain your reasons.**

4. **How do we see things if they don't give out light?**

We see things that are not light sources because they reflect light. Mirrors and metal foils reflect light so well that they behave like looking glass. Wood, paper and stones reflect enough light for us to see them but not enough light for us to see an image of ourselves.

Travelling light

Light travels in straight lines. You can see this when light comes through trees in the forest.

5. **What other evidence can you think of that shows light travels in straight lines?**

Your challenge ...

Things that do not give out light are seen because they reflect light from a light source. It would cost far too much money to put street lamps on every road. Find out what Catseyes are and how they work. Are they light sources?

BLOCKING OUT LIGHT

What's the big idea?

Objects are either opaque, transparent or translucent. An opaque object, with a light source, will make a definite shadow. Shadows are formed when the path of light is blocked.

The difference is ...

Bricks, thick card and wood are **opaque**. They do not let any light through them. Tissue paper, tracing paper and frosted glass are **translucent**. They let some light through. You cannot see clearly through something translucent. Windowpane glass and water are **transparent**. Transparent things let most of the light through, so you can see objects behind a glass windowpane clearly.

Windows in churches are often made of coloured (stained) glass. Although it is coloured, you can still see clearly through it.

1. **What would happen if stained glass windows were made of translucent glass?**

These children are making models of stained glass windows using card and paper. James is making parts of his window with coloured film used for lighting. Hannah is using tissue paper and Davinder is using coloured thick card.

2. **Whose model window will be opaque?**
3. **Can you decide which window will be translucent and which transparent?**

Big mistakes

Just because something is transparent does not mean it has no colour. If you take water and add a drop of food dye to it, the liquid is still transparent.

It is not only transparent materials that let light through.

4. Describe the difference between a transparent material and a translucent material.

With a bathroom window, people like light to get in, but they do not want to be seen.

5. Are bathroom windows usually opaque, transparent or translucent?

6. Which type of material makes the clearest shadows?

Opaque objects make clear shadows because they block out all the light. Light travels in straight lines and so the shape of the shadow will be the same as the shape of the opaque object.

Your challenge ...

Some people believe that shadows are made when solid objects block the light. This is not completely correct. Explain, using as much evidence as you can, why this is not completely correct.

FINDING OUT ABOUT SHADOWS

What's the big idea?

Shadows get bigger as the light source gets closer.

Puppet theatre

Sarah and Michael have made a shadow puppet theatre.

1. What do you think this puppet theatre is made from?
2. How do you think it works?

3. What is the light source for their theatre?

They have attached sticks to cardboard puppets to move them around. They have made a tracing paper screen. The other children watching can see the shadows. The frame of the puppet theatre is made of wood.

4. Which parts of the puppet theatre are translucent?
5. Which parts are opaque?
6. Why have the children chosen these materials?

Making big and small shadows

In the puppet theatre, moving the puppet closer to the torch makes the shadow change size.

7. How do you think the size will change?
8. What will make the shadow bigger?
9. What will make the shadow smaller? Why?

Remember: a shadow is made when an object blocks the light.

10. Design an investigation to show how moving the shadow puppet closer to the torch or closer to the screen affects the size of the shadow.

Think about the following:

- What will you need to measure?
- What will you keep the same?
- How will you record your results?

Your challenge ...

Imagine the torch can be moved to the left and right.
How will the shadow of a puppet change?
How will the shadow change if the torch is moved up and down?

Light and Shadows

SUNDIALS

What's the big idea?

The Sun seems to move across the sky as the Earth spins. The Sun is highest at around midday. The higher the sun in the sky, the shorter the shadows it casts.

Shadow clocks

Before mechanical clocks, people used the Sun to measure time.

Look at the numbers round the edge of the sundials.

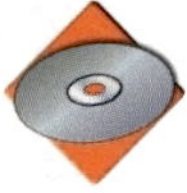

1. **What differences are there between how these numbers are arranged and how the numbers are marked on an analogue clock?**
2. **Why do you think they are set out differently?**
3. **Are all sundials set out the same?**
4. **What other interesting features do you notice?**

What moves?

Each morning, it starts to get light and then the Sun rises in the East. At about midday, the Sun is at its highest.

5. In approximately what direction does the Sun set?
6. In what direction is the Sun in the middle of the day?

The sun setting

Although the Sun seems to move across the sky, it is really the Earth that is moving. You can see how this happens by using yourself as a model.

Stand facing a friend. Hold up one finger in front of your face and look straight at the finger. Then turn round slowly but keep looking at your finger. Your friend seems to be moving around you, but it is you who is moving!

Our planet spins in the same way. The Sun stays in the same place, but because the Earth is spinning, it seems to be moving, just as your friend seemed to move.

Your challenge ...

Find out why the shadow stick on a sundial (the 'gnomon') is not vertical.

SHADOW PUPPET THEATRE

What's the big idea?

Scientific ideas are employed in many things that we use.
We use the properties of materials to choose suitable materials for a purpose.

Making light work

The behaviour of light can be used to entertain and create illusions. Here is a shadow puppet theatre. Think about how it works.

Shadow puppets, Bali

In the shadow puppet theatre, there is an opaque frame and a translucent screen. The puppets are behind the screen.

1. Where is the light source?

2. Design your own shadow puppet theatre. Work in a group and agree what to do. Your teacher will tell you what light source to use.

You need to think about what the theatre will be made from.

- What will the screen and frame be made from? What properties of the materials are important for this?
- What will the puppets be made from? What properties of the materials are important?
- Will the puppets be decorated?
- How will you move the puppets?

Write a short script to present a shadow puppet show to the rest of your class.

Special effects

Shiny materials form images. Mirrors and other shiny surfaces have often been used for special effects in theatres, magic shows and films.

In Victorian times theatres used a special effect called **Pepper's Ghost**. A huge sheet of polished glass was placed at an angle on the stage. The audience could not see the glass. Below the stage was an actor. The audience could not see the actor. The actor's reflected image in the glass looked like a ghost.

3. What properties of glass make it the best material for this trick?

Your challenge ...

Research some other ways that mirrors and shiny materials can be used to play tricks, for special effects or for serious purposes.

Glossary

absorbent	takes up water (or other liquids)
aluminium	silver-coloured metal that is very light
artificial	made by people; not natural
bacteria	types of tiny organism
carnivore	animal that eats only animals
compress	make shorter or smaller (by pushing)
copper	reddish coloured metal, used for making electrical wires
diet	the food that an animal normally eats
elastic (adjective)	can be extended or compressed, but will return to the original length
extend	make longer (by pulling)
flexible	bends easily without breaking
flower	part of a plant that produces seeds
fruit	seed case that develops from parts of the flower of a plant
hard	difficult to scratch
herbivore	animal that eats only plants
humus	dead animal and plant material in soil
igneous	type of rock made when molten rock cools
image	the likeness of something reflected from a shiny surface
magnetic	attracted to a magnet
metamorphic	type of rock formed from either sedimentary or igneous rock and changed by being further heated and/or compressed
natural	found in nature; not artificial
nutrient	material that an organism needs for growth and to remain healthy
omnivore	animal that eats both plants and animals
opaque	lets no light through
organism	any living thing
permeable	able to absorb water (or any liquid or gas)
plaque	mixture of food particles and bacteria that forms on teeth
polythene	type of plastic that is often flexible, used for making plastic shopping bags
repel	push away
rigid	not flexible; does not bend
root	part of a plant that anchors it and takes in water and mineral nutrients
sedimentary	type of rock formed when layers of rock particles are pressed together
shiny	reflects a lot of light
soil	material made from tiny rock particles, humus and water. Clay, sand and silt have different sizes of rock particles
starches	group of foods of vegetable origin, such as potato and cereals, that provide energy
stem	part of a plant that carries water and nutrients from the roots to other parts of the plant
strong	difficult to break
translucent	lets some light through, but is not clear
transparent	lets most of the light through and is clear